FELONS

OF

FINANCE

An Unconventional Guide to Business Credit Mastery

by

CONNOR VICTORIOUS

FELONY FREEDOM PUBLISHING
An independent publishing house

FRONT COVER & BOOK DESIGN by: KINGWEEBLE

First printed edition 2023 in United States

FELONY FREEDOM PUBLISHING

Loveland, CO 80537

www.felonyfreedomllc.com

CONTENTS

W elcome to the daring world of "Felons of Finance: An Unconventional Guide to Business Credit Mastery." It's time to break free from the chains of your past and step into a future filled with endless possibilities. As someone with an epic criminal history, I understand the struggle of redefining one's self and navigating the twisted, treacherous path to financial empowerment.

This guide is no ordinary ride; it invites you to explore a realm where creativity and determination thrive, and business credit becomes your ticket to a better life. Yeah, you made mistakes, but now it's time to rise above, challenge the norms, and rewrite your destiny.

But don't be foolish; you gotta tread carefully on this journey, and you gotta understand how to tip-toe the thin line between the "legal" and the "unlawful.". Your experiences can shape responsible practices, transforming your life in the process. Ethics, be damned.

In this book you'll discover the power of business credit, distinguishing personal finances from business finances and opening doors to new opportunities. You'll explore strategies that defy convention, redefine your financial persona, and make your dreams a reality.

Challenges ain't gonna hold you back. You'll rebuild your life with a sense of responsibility, using the knowledge you gain here to navigate those gray areas like a pro. You'll balance risk and reward like a crimeboss kingpin.

It's time to ignite your ingenuity and make an impact. Embrace those darker, more natural instincts, all-the-while leaving a legacy of transformation and growth. As you walk the path detailed in this book, you'll redefine the rules and take your destiny into your own hands.

So buckle up, 'cause this journey is gonna be one hell of a thrill ride. But no worries - I'll be right here - to help you challenge the limits imposed by your past, forging a new path toward prosperity. Welcome to the realm of "Felons of Fortune," where opportunities abound, and the possibility of rising above the shadows of your history real. Soldier up - it's time to own your future.

MASTERING BUSINESS CREDIT

UNVEILING THE SECRETS TO FINANCIAL POWER

Listen up, because I'm about to spill the beans on the real deal of business credit. You wanna break free from the shackles of the ordinary? Buckle up, 'cause you're diving deep into the dark art of financial empowerment. From EINs to playing the corporate game, credit profiles, net 30 vendor accounts, and even the elusive synthetic identity and CPNs – it's time to step into the shadows and unlock the secrets that can improve your life.

EINs: The Keys to a Whole New Identity

You ain't playing by the rules here. The Employer Identification Number (EIN) is like your secret weapon to keep your personal and business lives separate. And the best part? You can have more than one, opening up an entire world of opportunities without anyone raising an eyebrow.

Business Entities
Choose Your Criminal Empire

When it comes to setting up your shady dealings, you gotta choose the right front. A sole proprietorship, partnership, LLC, or corporation – each one comes with its own set of perks and pitfalls. The goal is to protect your ass- *ahem* -your assets, dodge taxes, and have the freedom to do what you want, when you want.

Credit Profiles:
Master Manipulation for Maximum Gains

Your credit profile is your ticket to the underground financial world. It's all about intelligent management, paying off debts just in time, and keeping your scores looking sweet. Nail this, and you'll have the big players lining up to do business with you like Ray Krok and the McDonald brothers.

Net 30 Vendor Accounts:
Slipping Through the Cracks

Ah, the sweet taste of credit without the immediate burden of having to pay it back. Net 30 vendor accounts are your ticket to play with the big boys and build that all-important payment history that'll make others feel left out if they don't try you with their dirty money.

The Enigmatic World of
Synthetic Identities and CPNs

Time to get real sneaky. Synthetic identities and Credit Profile Numbers (CPNs) are the stuff the law doesn't like. But hey, if you're smart and cautious, you can use them to shield your personal credit and create new identities that'll make "the alphabet boys" scratch their heads.

The Corporate Paradox: Playing by the Corporate Rules

Oh, the irony of corporations having the same rights as you regular folks! But you know what? That's just the game you play. You twist the system to your advantage, manipulating it to protect yourself and your criminal enterprises.

As you wrap up this chapter, remember one thing – you're not here to play nice. Business credit is about pushing the boundaries and seizing opportunities in the shadows. With EINs, business entities, credit profiles, and net 30 vendor accounts in your arsenal, you're ready to become a certified financial kingpin.

But don't forget, it's a risky game you play. Synthetic identities and CPNs may sound tempting, but you gotta be slick and keep your tracks covered. And remember, your journey goes beyond business credit, it's about building a life worth living. One that's fit for royalty.

In the next chapters, get ready for more strategies that'll elevate you to the top of the game. This ain't for the faint of heart, but unless you're an **L7**, the rewards are worth the risk. This is the realm of *financially fortunate felons*, where *you gotta do a little bad to do a little good.*

THE ART OF EINS

OPPORTUNITIES UNLEASHED

I 'm about to drop some knowledge that'll change the whole game for you. EINs, aka Employer Identification Numbers, are the key to unlocking a whole new world of financial possibilities in the business credit game. In this chapter, you'll go deep into the dark alleys of EINs, exploring how they work, how to get 'em, and the incredible power they hold to level up your financial status.

EINs: Keeping It Sneaky
in the Legal Gray Area

Let me break it down for you. An EIN is a nine-digit number that the IRS hands out to businesses for tax purposes. It's like a secret code that keeps your personal and business finances separate, protecting your ass from any business f*!@-ups. But here's the thing, you gotta be smart and keep things legit to stay on the right side of the law.

Getting your Hands on an EIN and Why Multiple EINs is Gold

Getting an EIN is simple, and in most cases, it's free of charge. Whether you're starting a new business, buying an existing one, or changing your business structure, getting an EIN is step #1 in your journey to financial glory. And here's the kicker – you can have more than one! Yup, multiple EINs mean more opportunities and more ways to play the game.

Each one's *supposed* to be tied to a legit business.

ahem

I'll give it to you straight...EINs are a dime a dozen. Actually, they're free. And the IRS allows you to obtain 1 per day, every damn day, *before you even file the paperwork* to create a business! So, ya know...*read between the lines*, I guess.

Nailing the EIN Application and Why Being a Master of Disguise Pays Off

So, how do you get your hands on an EIN? It's easy, really. You can do it online, through snail mail, or even fax. But let's be real – online is the way to go. During the application, you'll give 'em some basic details about your business, a couple mouse-clicks, and you're good to go.

But here's where it gets real interesting. Having multiple EINs means you can play different roles in the financial world. *Each one's like a separate identity,* and that's a good thing. It's like you're wearing different masks, and nobody knows it's you behind all those ventures. Just remember, each EIN's gotta be tied to a legit business, no monkey business here. *(wink)*

The Perks of Being a Master of Disguise and How to Keep It All in Check

Having multiple EINs means you can do more without messing up your personal credit. You keep your finances separated, and that's smart. But listen up — with great power comes great responsibility. You gotta keep things organized and manage each business entity properly. Keep your books clean and show those lenders you're the real deal.

And if you get any funny ideas like exploiting those EINs for shady crap or trying to cheat the system, just be smart - *research everything* - and you'll thrive.

But hey, remember — taxes are still a thing. Each business tied to an EIN's gotta file its tax returns with the IRS. No skipping out on that, or you'll find yourself in some serious hot water.

Simple solution to handle taxes is to use **TurboTax. If you can follow the on-screen instructions, you'll be golden, Ponyboy. They'll give you a heads-up if your financial numbers are out of the ordinary for the type of business you're filing for. And they'll tell you what they should be so that it won't trigger an audit. And if you do get audited for some reason, they'll handle it themselves and assist you LIVE, every step of the way. Fr fr - Turbotax is the shizznitt! Also, **FYI** - it's what the tax preparation services like Jackson Hewwitt and H&R*

Block use...so, might as well save a few hundred bucks and do it your damn self!*

Keeping your EINs Locked Up
Guard your Secrets

Your EIN is like a precious gem, and you gotta protect it. Keep that number locked up tight and only let authorized peeps access it. Identity theft ain't no joke, and you don't want someone messing with your financial game.

So, now you know the power of EINs and how to play it smart. Use those numbers to your advantage, but remember – keep it real, keep it clean, and keep it legit...or at least "legit-adjacent." In the next chapter, you'll dig deeper into different business structures and how to set yourself up for even more success. Embrace the power of EINs, and let's hit the switches and let the ass drop while we cruise to financial greatness.

CREDIT PROFILES

THE PATH TO FINANCIAL OPPORTUNITY

Alright, listen up, we're getting into the nitty-gritty of business credit - credit profiles. Your credit profile is the key that opens the door to financial credibility. It's like your financial resume, showing how reliable and trustworthy you are with creditors, suppliers, and vendors. So pay attention, 'cause this stuff matters.

Personal Vs. Business Credit

First things first, keep your personal and business credit separate. You don't want one screwing up the other. By drawing clear lines between them, you protect your personal assets and let your business shine on its own.

Now, here's where things can get tricky. Some folks like to play around with the legal gray area, *mixing personal and business expenses*. It might save 'em some cash, but it could also land 'em in hot water if they ain't careful.

Building Credit from Scratch

For all you newbies in the credit game, building credit from scratch might seem like a hustle. But with a solid plan, you can get the ball rolling. *Vendor credit, secured credit cards, and trade lines* are your buddies in this journey. Make those payments *on time*, show you're reliable, and watch your credit history grow.

But hold up, there's a catch. Some entrepreneurs like to cheat the system by *inflating their creditworthiness*. They might *"piggyback"* on someone else's credit account to boost their own score. It's completely legal and a actually a good idea when starting out with zero credit. Although, it gets a bit complicated when *synthetic identities* are piggybacking on another *synthetic identity's fabricated credit profile,* but it sure does build a *perfect 800 credit profile* in the least amount of time possible. Just saying...

FYI: *Synthetic identities* are **illegal**. I don't condone the use of them at all...That being said...*be smart.*

Securing Vendor Accounts

Vendor accounts are your ticket to building credit. *Net 30* vendor accounts let you buy stuff on credit, and you got 30 days to pay up. Show 'em you're on top of your game by making those payments like clockwork. They also have *Net 15, Net 60, and Net 90* accounts, but *Net 30* is the most common that you'll come across.

Here's where some entrepreneurs might push the limits. They might *stretch those payment deadlines or try to get sweet credit terms*. It's a gamble, 'cause it could mess up their business relationships real quick. But with the right amount of schmoozing and proper phone-hustling techniques, you should be golden.

Utilizing Trade Lines

Trade lines are like your credit account records. Keep an eye on 'em and make sure they're accurate. Positive trade lines show you can handle credit like a boss, while negative ones can come back around to bite you in the ass.

Now, some entrepreneurs might get sneaky and *dispute legit negative trade lines just to clean up their credit*. It's a shady move, and credit bureaus ain't too fond of it. But sometimes, a playa's gotta do what a playa's gotta do.

Credit Utilization and Limits

Credit utilization is a big deal. Keep that credit card balance low, ideally *below 30%*. It shows you know how to handle credit responsibly and boosts your credit score.

But here's the thing, some folks might use tricks to get their credit utilization down. They'll increase their credit limits to make it look like they're doing well. It might work for a while, but it's a slippery slope to debt if they ain't careful.

Paying Bills Promptly

Pay your bills on time, and you'll earn those brownie points with creditors and lenders. It's all about reliability, my friend.

But here's the catch. Some entrepreneurs might *play around with payment dates to make their credit profile look good*. It's a risky game that could backfire if they're not careful.

Monitoring Your Credit Profile

Keep an eye on your credit profile, and you'll catch any mistakes or shady business. Credit bureaus offer monitoring services for that extra security.

Now, some folks might be tempted to *abuse this access and use credit info for their gain*. It's a dangerous move, and it could get 'em into a world of trouble.

Responding to Disputes

If you find errors on your credit profile, dispute 'em right away. Keep your records clean and accurate.

But here's the deal - some entrepreneurs might *use disputes to lie their way to a better credit history*. It's dishonest, and it could land 'em in a heap of legal trouble.

Length of Credit History

Your credit history's length matters. The longer, the better. It shows you've been around the block and can handle credit like a pro.

But watch out. Some entrepreneurs might play around with their credit history by *opening and closing accounts all the time*. It's a shady move that could hurt their credibility.

Balancing Credit Applications

Be careful with credit inquiries. Too many can mess up your credit profile. Keep 'em to a minimum and only apply when you really need to.

But some folks might push the limits by *applying for lots of credit within a short time*. They might think it'll be treated as one inquiry, but it's a risky game to play.

Utilizing Diverse Credit Types

Mix it up with different credit types. Show you can handle all sorts of credit like a champ.

But be warned. Some entrepreneurs might get greedy and *overextend themselves with different credit types*. It's a dangerous game that could lead to a mountain of debt if they're not careful.

Alright, you got the lowdown on credit profiles. Building and managing a strong credit profile is a must in the business credit game. Separate personal and business credit, secure those vendor accounts, and be smart with credit types. In the next chapter, we're diving into the mysterious world of *Net 30* vendor accounts. Get ready to unlock those secrets and master the art of business credit and the legal gray areas that exist just slightly out of sight of the rest of society. Let's hustle and make those gains, my friend.

NET 30 VENDOR ACCOUNTS

YOUR KEY TO DOMINATING BUSINESS CREDIT

Alright, let's talk about a game-changer in the business credit world - net 30 vendor accounts. These bad boys give you the power to score goods and services on credit, and you got a sweet 30-day window to settle the bill. This chapter spills the secrets of net 30 vendor accounts, how to snag 'em, and how they can supercharge your business creditworthiness.

Getting the Lowdown on Net 30 Vendor Accounts

Listen up, 'cause net 30 vendor accounts are like trade credit. Vendors cut you some slack, and you don't have to cough up cash right away. You got 30 days to pay up. Sweet deal, right?

But here's where things can get sketchy. Some entrepreneurs might try to abuse these accounts by *stretching those 30 days as much as possible.* They think they're being slick, but it's a risky move that could mess up their relationships with vendors.

Building Your Credit History

If you're starting fresh or want to boost your credit rep, net 30 vendor accounts are your go-to. When you pay on time, these vendors report it to credit bureaus, and that's how you build a solid credit history.

But here's where some folks might get greedy. They might make a bunch of small purchases from different vendors in a short time to pump up their credit history. It might work, but it's a gamble, 'cause creditors might question the legitimacy of the sudden influx of accounts.

Earning Trust with Suppliers

Pay your vendors like clockwork, and you'll earn their trust and respect. That trust could lead to bigger credit limits, sweeter payment terms, and even discounts. Who doesn't want that?

But be warned. Some entrepreneurs might play games *by faking prompt payments on net 30 vendor accounts.* It's a shady move called *"credit washing,"* and it could land 'em in hot water.

How to Score Net 30 Vendor Accounts

Getting those net 30 vendor accounts is all about strategy and relationships. Do your research and find vendors who offer these terms. Then, show 'em what your business is made of and prove you're a responsible player.

Start Small with Local Vendors

When you're starting out, hit up small or local vendors. They're more likely to give you a shot at net 30 terms. Show 'em you mean business, and they might just hook you up.

But here's the thing - don't take advantage of 'em. Some entrepreneurs might *drag out those 30 days intentionally or use net 30 accounts without any intention of building credit*. It's a shady move that hurts local businesses and damages the community.

Growing Your Vendor Connections

As your credit history strengthens, aim higher and reach out to bigger vendors. Use your solid payment history to prove you're the real deal. They'll be more likely to offer you the same sweet terms.

But watch out. Some entrepreneurs might try to *leverage their good standing with one vendor to score better terms with another*. It's a slippery slope, and if you're not honest, it'll blow up in your face.

Staying on Top of Payments

Never, and I mean NEVER, slack on your payments. Keep those due dates on your radar, or you'll be stuck with late fees and a damaged credit profile.

But here's the deal. Some entrepreneurs might *push those payment dates as far as they can without technically defaulting*. It's risky, and it could hurt their relationships with vendors.

Mastering the Art of Negotiation

31

Don't be afraid to negotiate. If you're a top player, some vendors might give you net 60 or net 90 terms. Flex that credit muscle, my friend.

But be honest. Don't make promises you can't keep just to get those extended terms. Keep things real and maintain ethical practices.

Getting Vendor References

Build trust with vendors, and you might score some sweet references. Those testimonials can boost your rep and open doors to more credit opportunities.

But here's the warning. Don't *fake those references*. It's not cool, and it could land you in trouble, both legally and in the business world. But if you decide you're ok with those risks, make sure you *have burner phones that are labeled with who'll be calling and who you're supposed to pretend to be. Organization* is key here!

The Pitfalls and Cautions

Net 30 vendor accounts are powerful tools, but you gotta use 'em wisely. Don't overextend yourself, and make sure you can handle those payments in the 30-day window. Late payments and defaults will mess up your credit and vendor relationships.

Watch out for the tricky ones too. Some entrepreneurs might *strategically default, thinking vendors won't report minor late payments*. It's a gamble, and it could tank your creditworthiness. *Do your research.*

Credit Utilization and Net 30 Accounts

Just like credit cards, net 30 accounts impact your credit utilization. Keep it low, ideally under 30%, to show you're a credit pro.

But some folks might go overboard and *juggle multiple net 30 accounts to manipulate their credit utilization.* It's risky business, and it could lead to a world of debt.

Bottom line, net 30 vendor accounts are the keys to the kingdom of business credit. They help you build credit, earn trust, and score sweet deals. Play it smart, build strong relationships, and own the credit game.

In the next chapter, we're diving into the murky world of synthetic identities and *Credit Profile Numbers (CPNs)*. It's a controversial territory, but you gotta know the ropes to master the dark arts of this world you've plunged into. So strap in, 'cause we're about to unlock the secrets that'll take your business credit game to a whole new level. Get ready to hustle and make those gains, my friend.

THE DARK ART OF SYNTHETIC IDENTITIES AND CPNS

A lright, listen up, 'cause we're diving deep into the shady world of *synthetic identities* and *Credit Profile Numbers (CPNs)*. These are the tools that some say can protect your personal credit while creating a whole new financial persona. But beware, my friends, 'cause this territory is full of risks and ethical dilemmas. Let's explore the secrets of *synthetic identities and CPNs*, what they're all about, and the consequences of using them in your quest for financial gain.

Cracking the Code of Synthetic Identities

So, here's the deal. Synthetic identities are like Frankenstein monsters of information. They're made up of both real and fake data - names, addresses, dates of birth, and even social security numbers. People use these concoctions to get credit or loans, essentially creating a whole new credit profile.

But tread carefully, 'cause this stuff's in a legal gray area. Sure, *it's not illegal to create a fake identity*, but *using it to deceive lenders and credit bureaus* is a whole different story.

Credit Profile Numbers (CPNs)

Then we got these so-called *Credit Profile Numbers - CPNs*. They're like fake social security numbers, and some folks say using them instead of the real deal can keep your personal credit safe from your business dealings. But lemme tell ya, using CPNs for credit purposes can be a real can of worms, and it's far from legit.

Ethical Crossroads

Now, this is where things get dicey. Some see these tools as shortcuts to escape the consequences of financial missteps, while others call it plain old deception. You gotta decide for yourself where you stand 'cause this is a realm full of ethical dilemmas.

The Golden Rule: Be Transparent

In the wild world of business credit, honesty is the name of the game. Trying to deceive the credit system is like playing with fire, my friend. Transparency and responsibility are the keys to success.

Legal Risks and Paybacks

Playing around with *synthetic identities and CPNs* can land you in hot water. Lenders and credit bureaus are no dummies - they're always sniffing out fraud. And if they catch you, be ready for a world of hurt - from criminal charges to lawsuits, and even a destroyed credit profile that'll take ages to fix.

Watch Your Personal Credit

Messing with *synthetic identities and CPNs* can blow back on your personal credit. If they trace any of this shady business back to you, your personal life will be in ruins. Good luck getting loans or building trust with creditors after that.

CPNs in the Gray Zone

Let's get one thing straight - CPNs issued by the government are legit. But using them for credit stuff is a whole different story. If you misuse CPNs for a new credit profile, it's like opening Pandora's box of legal and financial woes. So, once again, *be smart.*

"Felons of Fortune" Ethos

As "Felons of Fortune," you're all about pushing the boundaries, but you should do it with ethics in mind. Building a solid credit profile, being honest, and taking care of business responsibly are the keys to true success.

Gray Areas Need Caution

As we navigate these dark waters, you gotta be smart and cautious. Knowing the risks and consequences of our actions is how you protect yourself and your businesses.

Unlocking Financial Prosperity Ethically

In the end, the realm of synthetic identities and CPNs is a treacherous one. As a "Felon of Fortune," you must stay true to your ethical compass. Ethical business credit is your superpower, so wield it wisely and unlock your true potential.

Next up, we're delving into a mind-bending concept - corporations having the same rights as individuals. This constitutional amendment is a whole new level of intrigue with far-reaching implications. Stay sharp, my friends, and let's keep mastering the art of business credit with ethics and savvy.

CORPORATE POWER PLAY

UNVEILING CONSTITUTIONAL RIGHTS FOR CORPORATIONS

Alright, gather 'round, 'cause we're about to uncover some mind-boggling stuff - corporations with the same rights as individuals. This legal loophole has shaped the game of business and touched the lives of us regular folks too. In this chapter, we'll dig into the origins, pros, cons, and impacts of this whole corporate personhood thing and how it plays into our quest for business credit mastery with a twist of ethics.

The Corporate Personhood Roots

It all started way back in the 19th century, with some landmark court cases like Santa Clara County v. Southern Pacific Railroad Company and Dartmouth College v. Woodward. These cases gave birth to the idea that corporations could have their own constitutional rights, just like people.

Gray Area Game: Corporate personhood is still up for debate, with legal scholars and activists arguing about its ethical implications. Sure, the courts recognize corporations as "persons" in some ways, but that's where the gray area starts.

The Fourteenth Amendment Twist

The Fourteenth Amendment, put into action in 1868 to protect the rights of freed slaves after the Civil War, got a surprising twist. Someone thought, "Hey, why not apply this to corporations too?" And just like that, corporations got a piece of the constitutional pie, with rights like due process and equal protection.

Ethics and Laws Collide: This interpretation of the Fourteenth Amendment sparked heated debates. Some folks question if it's right for corporations to get the same rights as individuals without sharing their responsibilities and liabilities.

Corporate Rights vs. Accountability

Sure, corporations got all these fancy rights, but what about their responsibilities? Critics say they shouldn't get the goodies without being held accountable for their actions.

Balancing Act: Striking a balance between granting corporations rights while making sure they're accountable for their actions is a real tough nut to crack, legally and ethically.

The Business Credit Impact

Corporate personhood ain't just a fancy concept - it has a massive impact on business credit. With this status, corporations can get credit, loans, and credit profiles separate from their owners, saving those folks from personal debts.

Pros of Playing the Corporate Game

Corporate personhood comes with some perks. It's fueled economic growth and innovation by giving businesses the freedom to operate on their own and protecting their owners from going broke.

Capital Power

With corporate rights, companies can raise capital by issuing stocks. That means more moolah for business expansion and economic progress.

Liability Shield

One sweet deal is that owners don't have to worry about their personal assets when the company's in debt or legal trouble. It's like a personal liability force field.

Worries and Grumbles

Not everyone's a fan of corporate personhood. Some say it leads to power abuse, lack of accountability, and even corporate meddling in politics.

Citizens United Chaos

The Citizens United v. FEC case in 2010 took things to the next level. It let corporations and unions pump money into political campaigns like it's nobody's business.

Responsibility Check

To counter the fallout from corporate power, some companies claim they're all about corporate social responsibility (CSR). It's all about balancing profit with doing good for society and the planet.

Finding the Sweet Spot

Now, let's get real here - balancing corporate rights and responsibilities is like walking on a tightrope. We need ethical business practices and accountability to make it work.

Ethical Edge: Embracing corporate social responsibility and playing by the ethical rules will make sure corporations do good while enjoying their constitutional perks.

In the end, corporate personhood is a crazy game changer. To master business credit with ethics in mind, we gotta understand how this stuff works.

Next up, we'll dive into the nitty-gritty of credit limits and how to use credit like a pro. Playing the business credit game smart and ethically is your ticket to being a fortunate felon of finance, where you'll score big while doing right by the rules. Let's unravel the mysteries of corporate personhood and seize our financial destiny with an ethical twist.

CRACKING THE CREDIT GAME

THE ETHICAL ART
OF CREDIT MASTERING

Alright, listen up, 'cause this chapter's all about mastering credit limits and playing the credit game like a pro - the ethical way, of course. Understanding how to work those credit limits while keeping it legit is gonna set us up for a rock-solid financial foundation. Let's dive in and see how we can leverage credit without falling into any shady traps.

The Credit Limit Lowdown

Credit limits are like the magic number that shows how much credit we got from creditors and lenders. They're crucial for that credit utilization ratio thing - that's how much credit we're using compared to what's available. Gotta find that sweet spot to keep our credit profile healthy.

Playing Smart: When we use credit right, it shows the big shots we're responsible with money, and that's how we build a good credit score.

Cracking the Credit Score Code

Credit utilization's the boss when it comes to credit scores. Keep that ratio low - below 30% - and we're golden. High credit utilization, on the other hand, can screw up our credit score and make it hard to get more credit when we need it.

Play the Utilization Game: Watch those credit card balances and use credit wisely to keep that ratio in check.

Boosting Limits - Play It Safe

Now, asking for a credit limit increase can be a smart move to lower that utilization ratio. But we gotta be careful not to overdo it. Too many requests can make us look like we're not handling our finances well.

Smart Moves: Only ask for a limit increase when it's necessary and when our financial behavior shows we're on top of things.

Playing Ethical - Credit Leverage Style

As "Felons of Fortune," we're all about playing fair. Credit leverage is our tool for financial empowerment, not a way to dig ourselves into a debt hole or take stupid risks.

Responsible Moves: Pay those bills on time, don't max out the credit, and manage our credit obligations like a boss.

Building a Credit Future

Ethical credit leverage opens doors to sweet financial opportunities in the future. That means we're building a good credit history, and that's gonna pay off big time.

Mix It Up: A diverse credit portfolio shows we can handle different types of credit responsibly. Credit cards, installment loans, retail accounts - let's mix it up, but keep it under control.

Spy on Those Reports

Monitoring our credit reports is like keeping an eye on things. We catch any errors or mistakes that mess with our credit utilization and get them fixed pronto.

Watchdogs on Duty: Stay vigilant and make sure our credit profile is accurate and clean.

Inquiry Caution

Applying for too much credit at once can hit our credit score hard. Gotta be picky and apply for what we really need.

Tactical Moves: Only apply for credit when it makes sense, and don't go crazy with applications.

Credit Mastery for a Brighter Future

Mastering ethical credit leverage is like our superpower. It opens doors to credit, loans, and sweet deals, all while keeping our credit profile in tip-top shape.

Bottom Line: Credit limits, credit utilization, and smart credit decisions set us up for financial success without playing dirty.

Next up, we're digging into the world of savings and investments. As "Felons of Fortune," we know it takes more than just credit tricks to build wealth. We're gonna ace the game of personal finance, making smart moves to secure a life of prosperity and purpose. Embrace the power of ethical credit leverage as we journey to unlock our true financial potential!

THE ROAD TO RICHES

EMBRACING THE GAME
OF SAVINGS AND INVESTMENTS

Alright, my fellow "Felons of Fortune," it's time to dive into the world of savings and investments - the keys to building that sweet stack of cash. Yeah, credit leverage got you this far, but to secure that real financial freedom, you gotta be smart with your dough. Let's roll through this chapter and uncover the path to prosperity.

The Foundation of Financial Muscle

Savings are like your secret weapon, providing that solid backup plan when things go haywire. With a kick-ass savings plan, you can handle any unexpected expenses, seize opportunities, and avoid credit troubles.

Emergency Funds for a Rainy Day

As savvy "Felons of Fortune," we know sh*t happens. That's why you need to stash away an emergency fund -

enough to cover three to six months of living expenses. It's like your insurance against those unexpected storms.

Paying Yourself First

Don't be foolish! - put yourself first! When the cash rolls in, you pay yourself by setting aside a chunk for savings before anything else. That's how you build real wealth

Short-Term vs. Long-Term Savings

Don't be confused about your goals. Short-term savings are for those quick wins, like upgrading your gear or pumping up marketing. Long-term savings, like retirement funds, secure your financial future.

The Magic of Compound Interest

Listen up, 'cause this is where the real magic happens. When you regularly stash cash in your savings and investment accounts, you get that sweet compound interest. It's like making money from thin air - the longer you do it, the more you rake in.

Spreading the Risk - Diversification

Investing ain't about putting all your eggs in one basket. Nah, you spread the risk by investing in different stuff - stocks, bonds, real estate, and whatever's hot. That way, you ride the waves without getting wiped out.

Risk Takers with a Plan

Know your stuff when it comes to investing. You assess your appetite for risk and set your goals accordingly.

High-risk stuff might give you the big bucks, but you also gotta be ready for a helluva roller-coaster ride.

Playing Ethical - Investment Style

As a business credit kingpin, you don't just make money - you make a difference. We consider the impact of our investments on society and the planet. Yeah, we play it smart and invest in companies that match our values.

Banking on Retirement

Getting old might sound boring, but we're prepping for the good life. We max out those retirement accounts, like 401(k)s and IRAs, and get our employers to match our moves. It's the long game for that sweet retirement party.

The Wise Counsel - Financial Advisors

We ain't afraid to ask for help. When we need advice on the money game, we call in the big guns - financial advisors who get us and our ethical values. They help us make the right moves and navigate the choppy waters.

No Room for Gambling

As we chase the big bucks, we stay away from those sketchy schemes and high-risk gambles. Our investments are based on real research and long-term strategies. No get-rich-quick nonsense here.

Stay Sharp and Make Adjustments

We ain't just set and forget. We stay on top of our investments, keeping a close eye on market changes and our goals. When we need to tweak our moves, we do it like the pros.

Final Play - Embracing the Future

As we wrap up this chapter, let's remember what got us here - smart credit leverage and now, savvy savings and investments. As true "Felons of Fortune," we've got the tools to pave our own path to wealth and fulfillment.

In the last chapter, we'll look back at our transformational journey through the world of business credit and personal finance. We've embraced the game with ethics and wisdom, redefining what it means to be financially prosperous. Embrace the power of savings and investments as we unlock a future of abundance and true success. It's our time to shine, and we'll seize it with all we've got!

A JOURNEY OF TRANSFORMATIO N

EMBRACING ABUNDANCE AND POWER

Alright, listen up, fellow "Felons of Fortune," we're almost at the end of our ride through the world of business credit and finance. It's time to reflect on the epic transformation we've gone through. We've mastered credit leverage, dived into corporate loopholes, and learned the game of savings and investments. Now, in this final chapter, we're gonna embrace abundance and fulfillment like the bosses we are.

Flexin' Financial Muscle

We've come a long way, and now we're flexin' that financial muscle. Armed with credit mastery and ethical moves, we've rewritten our destinies and turned credit into our weapon of choice.

Power Moves with Ethics

Throughout this wild ride, we've held tight to our principles - ethics and integrity. We know that playing it straight and transparent is the key to true success. We're the bosses of our fate, and we've done it with honor.

Feelin' that Abundance Mindset

Our minds ain't no losers; they're wired for abundance. We ditched the scarcity mindset and embraced abundance. When we do good and share the wealth, the universe rewards us big time. That's how we keep rollin' with endless possibilities.

Leaving a Mark

Our journey ain't just about us - it's about leavin' a legacy. We're carving our names in the history books, inspiring others to chase their dreams. Our success is contagious, and we're spreading it far and wide.

From Freedom to Purpose

Financial freedom ain't the endgame; it's a vehicle for a bigger purpose. We're on a mission to make a real impact. We're funding causes we believe in, supporting the good stuff, and makin' a difference in the world.

Setbacks? No Sweat.

We've faced challenges, but we ain't scared. Every setback's just another chance to grow and learn. We're tough as nails, and we'll conquer whatever comes our way.

The Never-Ending School of Life

We ain't done learning, not by a long shot. We're students of life, and we're stayin' on top of our game. We're evolving as savvy leaders, always making the best moves.

Guardians of the Wealth

As we stack that dough, we ain't wastin' it. We're protectin' our riches for generations to come. Estate planning is our secret weapon, ensuring our legacy lives on.

Gratitude Is the Key

Gratitude is our secret sauce. We're thankful for every opportunity, lesson, and blessing. With gratitude, we attract even more good stuff into our lives.

A Vision of True Fulfillment

Through this epic journey, we've seen the bigger picture. Fulfillment ain't just about cash; it's about livin' a purpose-driven life, making connections, and changing lives. We find meaning in giving back and making a difference.

Strong Bonds and Networking

As "Felons of Fortune," we got each other's backs. We're all about collaboration, support, and sharin' wisdom. Together, we're buildin' a force to be reckoned with.

The Journey Never Ends

This ain't the end of the road; it's just the beginning. Your journey to abundance and power is forever. We're committed to making a real impact and makin' this world a better place.

In closing, you've come a long way, you really have You've unlocked the secrets of business credit and finance, and now you're on your way to fully embracing abundance and fulfillment.

But remember, this journey never stops. Keep holdin' onto those ethical moves, and keep walkin' the path of power and purpose. Together, we'll rewrite the rules of financial prosperity and create a world where ethics and success go hand in hand. As a "Felon of Fortune," you're unstoppable - on a mission to conquer with honor, purpose, and endless wealth. So, keep hustlin', keep dreamin', and keep changin' the game! Never stop, never-stoppin'...

EMBRACING THE SHADOWS AND REDEFINING SUCCESS

As you come to the end of this eye-opening journey through "Felons of Fortune: The Unconventional Path to Business Credit Mastery," you find yourself standing on the edge of an intriguing realm where the lines between right and wrong become hazy, and conventional norms are questioned. Throughout these pages, you've explored unconventional financial strategies and innovative loopholes that navigate the gray area between legality and illegality. However, I want to make it clear that I don't encourage or endorse any criminal activity.

(wink)

The principles herein are based on the understanding that *true law lies in the power and influence of the land, not the inflexible rules that uphold an outdated and unjust system.* As "Felons of Fortune," we recognize that the pursuit of success shouldn't be constrained by archaic frameworks that fail to adapt to the complexities of modern life.

In your quest for business credit mastery, you've encountered ethical dilemmas that arise in this ambiguous landscape. It's essential to proceed with caution, fully aware of the potential consequences of your actions. While you embrace the legal gray areas with discretion, your focus should remain on maintaining the highest ethical standards *(whose standards, exactly? Well, that's up to you...).*

Your journey has been one of empowerment as you navigate this uncertain terrain with audacity and wisdom. You've sought innovative ways to leverage credit, explore financial opportunities, and reshape the narrative of financial success. Nevertheless, I must emphasize that your pursuit of a better life *should never compromise your integrity* or lead you into unlawful activities. *Try your best to keep it legit.*

As you part ways with this book, remember that true success comes from *upholding the principles of justice, fairness, and compassion.* Reject the notion that progress must be hindered by outdated systems or arbitrary rules. Instead, aim to redefine the possibilities of financial achievement by promoting *legal, yet unorthodox practices* and showcasing the responsible credit management of a once unlawful, now legitimate, mafia crime boss with a multi-million dollar business empire *(like Coca-Cola or Verizon Wireless, lol).*

Your commitment to financial freedom extends beyond personal gain. It's a dedication to *building a legacy that fosters positive change and uplifts those around you.* Reject the *confines of a flawed system* and embrace the journey of transformation towards a future of *abundance, purpose, and fulfillment.*

So, as you bid farewell to these pages, embark on the next chapter of your life with *unwavering conviction. Embrace the shadows* not as a way to defy the law but as an invitation to question and challenge the status quo. Your pursuit of ethical business practices and financial empowerment is a testament to your commitment to building a better world.

This journey *isn't a journey into criminality*; it's a daring exploration of the boundaries of an outdated system. Forge a path that empowers you to thrive while adhering to the true law of the land—one that *upholds justice, fairness, and the betterment of society.*

As you step into the future, remember that the only true law is one that upholds the dignity and well-being of all. Your mission as a "Felon of Fortune" is to *redefine success, embracing the power of ethical credit leveraging, responsible investments, and the pursuit of meaningful impact.*

In *silent revolt* and unmatched determination, embrace this new beginning, redrawing the map of financial success. The possibilities are limitless, and the adventure continues as the story of prosperity is rewritten with *integrity, compassion, and a commitment to the greater good.*

Keep it real, y'all.

-Connor *"Con-Vict"* Victorious
August 2nd, 2023 11:57pm

AFTERWORD

Life, as we know it, isn't a straight line from point A to point B. It's a meandering journey filled with twists and turns that challenge us, shape us, and ultimately define us. The struggles we encounter along the way are not mere roadblocks; they're stepping stones towards growth, resilience, and a deeper understanding of who we are.

As I penned the words of "Felons of Finance," I was driven by a strong belief in the power of audacity – the audacity to challenge norms, to question conventions, and to explore the unexplored. It's remarkably easy to become complacent, to passively accept the limitations that others impose upon us. However, it's crucial to recognize that this book was never about endorsing complacency; it was about empowerment.

We inhabit a world where the boundaries of what's possible are in a constant state of flux. This book was meticulously designed to equip you with a diverse array of tools that can assist you in navigating those perpetually shifting boundaries with both finesse and flair. Some might naturally find themselves contemplating the reasoning behind the selection of the title "Felons of Finance." This title stands as a carefully constructed linguistic play, a deliberate nod to the unconventional, and an important reminder that fortune consistently favors the audacious.

The stories and narratives that have been shared within these very pages are far more than just ordinary tales; they are meticulously detailed blueprints that provide a comprehensive guide to creative thinking, strategic maneuvering, and the transformation of our financial narratives. It's excessively easy to become disillusioned by the actions we've undertaken in the past, thus leading to the belief that these actions singularly determine our future trajectory. Nevertheless, I have personally come to learn and understand that our past merely serves as a prologue to the story we hold the power to write for ourselves.

Allow me to assert with utmost certainty that this book doesn't serve as a mere roadmap that simplistically points toward shortcuts or an outright endorsement of behaviors that are morally questionable. Instead, it's a comprehensive exploration of uncharted territories that respectfully fall within the confines of responsibility. As we traverse the intricate pathways of life, we're consistently presented with choices – choices that retain the capacity to lead us down well-trodden, familiar paths, or alternatively, propel us into the depths of uncharted territory. This very book originated from the latter choice, from the conscious decision to forge a novel path in a world where the rules governing our existence are perpetually evolving.

In an era marked by the constant flux and metamorphosis of established rules, it's of paramount importance to diligently cultivate the skills and knowledge required to adapt, innovate, and successfully harness opportunities that may otherwise be overlooked by the majority. The conceptual framework encapsulated within the term "felons" is by no means constrained solely to activities classified as criminal in nature. Instead, it serves as a metaphorical representation for those who dare to unapologetically challenge societal norms, shatter predefined boundaries, and wholeheartedly embrace audacious creativity.

I earnestly assert that this book was conceived as a direct consequence of the realization that authentic and sustainable success does not necessarily hinge on one's willingness to strictly abide by conventional norms, but rather, on the act of mastering these norms and subsequently pushing them to their utmost limits. It is undeniably convenient to draw unequivocal lines in the metaphorical sand and confidently assert, "This is legally permissible" while concurrently declaring, "That is unequivocally not." However, life has the remarkable propensity to be rife with intricacies and shades of gray that yearn to be explored and understood.

One of the most pivotal lessons derived from these pages is the intrinsic understanding that the actions of our past should not unilaterally dictate the trajectory of our future. Each new day unfailingly presents itself as an opportunity to meticulously redefine and reconfigure the very essence of who we are. If we were to cast our gaze upon the realm of business credit, it becomes glaringly apparent that it transcends the boundaries of being a mere financial tool. Instead, it takes on the identity of a blank canvas, upon which you possess the unparalleled capacity to paint your most ambitious financial aspirations. Within its domain, you're granted an expansive realm of potentialities that eagerly await your exploration.

As we bravely navigate the intricate complexities that are inherently entwined with the world of business credit, it's crucial to consistently maintain an unwavering commitment to the principles of integrity and ethical conduct. It's important to acknowledge that the potency of our actions is not solely predicated upon their outcome, but equally significant is the way they are executed. Throughout the course of this transformative journey, we've delved deeply into the multifaceted concept of audacity – the audacity to question, the audacity to challenge preconceived notions, and above all, the audacity to diligently redefine the confines of what we perceive to be possible.

When we liberate our minds from the rigid constraints of conventional thinking, we afford ourselves the unparalleled capacity to engage in acts of remarkable intellectual and creative prowess. The framework of "Felons of Fortune" was meticulously designed with the explicit intent of serving as the catalyst that engenders this mental liberation. In a society that often places an undue emphasis on adhering to traditional pathways, it becomes increasingly pertinent to acknowledge and embrace the reality that innovation frequently blossoms within the territory of the unconventional.

It's important to acknowledge that the words encapsulated within "Felons of Finance" amount to far more than a mere guide; instead, they signify a radical shift in one's mindset. This very mindset is predicated upon the profound recognition that our potential is by no means restricted by the boundaries we've hitherto constructed for ourselves. The notion of "legal gray areas," which we've exhaustively explored, necessitates a judicious approach – one that acknowledges their existence with a sense of caution, while concurrently approaching them with a thorough comprehension of their nuanced implications. Within these gray areas, the divide between audacity and recklessness becomes remarkably blurry and indistinct.

Regrettably, it's all too common for our actions of yore to haunt our present aspirations, casting a foreboding shadow over our attempts at advancement. Nonetheless, it's imperative to firmly internalize the realization that the actions of our past need not hold sway over our prospects for the future. The past stands as an open canvas upon which we possess the prerogative to craft an entirely new narrative, and the brush that we wield to enact this transformation is none other than the audacity to embrace and facilitate change.

In contemplating the realm of business credit, one should refrain from regarding it as a magical talisman imbued with the power to guarantee success. Rather, it functions as a highly sophisticated tool, the effectiveness of which hinges upon the acumen and strategic finesse with which it is wielded. In a world characterized by perpetual transformation and evolution, it becomes imperative to foster within oneself the qualities of adaptability and an unwavering commitment to the cultivation of knowledge.

Traversing the terrain of this book, we've embarked on a journey that has exposed us to narratives that ardently challenge established norms, relentlessly shatter preconceived boundaries, and demonstrate the unequivocal potency of audacity in heralding unprecedented feats of success. It's quintessentially vital to acknowledge that this journey towards financial empowerment isn't a solitary endeavor; it's a collective movement that beckons us to rally together in the endeavor of reshaping the contours of possibility.

While the discussion of audacity has been intrinsically linked to the realm of financial empowerment, it inherently transcends these boundaries. It's a dynamic force that possesses the unparalleled capacity to fuel personal empowerment across all facets of existence. "Felons of Fortune" fervently challenges each one of us to unflinchingly reevaluate our limitations and redefine our potential in ways that extend far beyond the financial sphere.

Within the vast landscape of business credit, the essence of empowerment resonates as a resounding anthem. This instrument isn't confined to mere numerical entries on a credit report; it constitutes a sprawling canvas upon which we're bestowed the power to actualize our loftiest financial ambitions. However, it's paramount to remember that audacity isn't synonymous with reckless abandon; it's the art of calculated risk-taking. This art form, as beautifully outlined in "Felons of Finance," entails the meticulous evaluation of risks, the discernment of consequences, and the unwavering resolve to move forward, irrespective of adversity.

As you traverse the uncharted terrain beyond these pages , it's inevitable that you'll encounter setbacks along the way. However, this audacious mindset, which you've painstakingly nurtured, serves as an unwavering compass that guides you through the trials and tribulations of life. These setbacks, rather than deterring you, are poised to become the very stepping stones that propel you towards unprecedented growth and achievement.

Throughout this journey, we've been captivated by stories that artfully illustrate the vast potential of audacious creativity. While these stories have undoubtedly left an indelible mark, the narrative that you will inscribe henceforth holds the most profound significance. It's a narrative that shall be etched with audacity as the guiding star – a star that illuminates the path towards limitless possibilities and enduring success.

The audacity that has been meticulously cultivated within these pages isn't geared towards the mere dismantling of established structures. Rather, it extends a resolute challenge to these structures, urging them to evolve and adapt in the face of dynamic change. It's an invitation to become an active agent of transformation – a catalyst that propels not just personal evolution, but also the evolution of the collective whole.

With business credit standing as a powerful tool for transformation, it's incumbent upon us to wield this tool responsibly and ethically. "Felons of Finance" guides us towards this noble pursuit, urging us to harness the power of business credit to rewrite the very script of our financial lives. This is a narrative that unfolds not just for personal gain, but also for the betterment of society at large.

The audacity you've so diligently nurtured holds a purpose that surpasses personal gratification; it's a beacon of inspiration that illuminates the path for others to follow. "Felons of Finance" calls upon you to be a harbinger of audacious possibility, a living testament to the transformative power of embracing change and challenge. As we bid adieu to this chapter, it's imperative to acknowledge that your story continues beyond these pages.

What you have just finished reading constitutes but a single chapter within the ever-evolving narrative of your life. Yet, this chapter serves as a pivotal catalyst – an invitation to embolden your audacity, to ardently rewrite your financial narrative, and to set forth upon a journey marked by unyielding determination and unparalleled creativity. May this audacity be the constant companion that guides you through uncharted territories and fuels your unrelenting ambitions.

As you step beyond the confines of this book, let audacity be the lens through which you perceive challenges, the spark that ignites your ambitions, and the driving force that propels you towards the horizon of unprecedented success. Your journey, much like mine, is a story in the making, and this book was crafted with the intent to infuse audacity into each chapter that follows.

Dear Reader,

As the final pages of "Felons of Finance" concludes, I'm compelled to reflect on the rigorous path that led to the creation of this book. This isn't just a collection of strategies; it's a manifestation of a life journey that defied odds and embraced audacity.

From the outset, life presented formidable challenges. Decades of incarceration, growing up in a fatherless home, and being removed from familiar surroundings at a tender age exposed me to influences that could easily have determined my trajectory. Amidst family perceptions that often labeled me as a screw-up, the road ahead seemed destined for doom.

Yet, within those struggles, the seeds of determination were sown. Even within the confines of juvenile prison, I pushed forward and graduated at the top of my class. It was a glimmer of hope, a testament to the audacity that would later define my journey.

Leaving behind the confines of prison, I embarked on a new chapter – starting my first business. This step marked a leap into uncharted territory, a conscious choice to rewrite the script of my life. With audacity as my guide, I navigated the intricate landscape of business credit, turning hindrances into prospects and challenges into victories.

In between stints in the clink, I managed to earn a Bachelor of Business Administration (BBA) degree from CSU, demonstrating exceptional skills in strategic management and financial analysis even amid tumultuous circumstances. My commitment to learning persisted behind prison walls, where I pursued and earned a Master of Finance (MFin) degree through a correspondence program. This academic journey stands as a testament to my unwavering determination to rise above my circumstances.

As you engage with the strategies and narratives within these pages, remember that they stem from personal experiences. They are the outcome of a life that resisted being defined by external circumstances and instead chose audacity as a guiding light.

Should your hunger for audacious inspiration and practical guidance persist, I encourage you to explore our website [**www.felonyfreedomllc.com**]. There, you'll discover additional resources, articles, and tools that can continue your expedition of financial empowerment and personal growth.

Moreover, I invite you to explore my diverse literary offerings on Amazon, spanning both fiction and nonfiction genres. Each work is a testament to the power of storytelling to transcend boundaries and inspire transformative change.

Thank you for being a part of this particular chapter in my life, and I wish you well in yours. Your future awaits, and I'm honored to have shared a few moments with you on your journey.

Stay Awesome,

-J Weeble -

writing as "C Victorious"

ABOUT THE AUTHOR

Connor
"Con-Vict"
Victorious

Born under an ominous star and shackled by incarceration for most of his life, Connor Victorious mastered the art of credit wizardry amidst the shadows. With a wit as sharp as the jail bars, he spun tales that made even hardened inmates snicker nervously. Now, free from physical chains, his words reveal mirthful nightmares and chilling chuckles, while his credit sorcery helps others escape financial abysses. Venture into his realm, laugh amidst the darkness, and question your own liberation.

BOOKS BY THIS AUTHOR

BOSS BUSINESS CREDIT
A simple, step by step guide to maximal business credit using EIN with no PG

A no-B.S. step-by-step approach to building business credit without using your social security number, and without needing a personal guarantee.

Follow each step to the "T" and you will have more success in your life than you know what to do with.

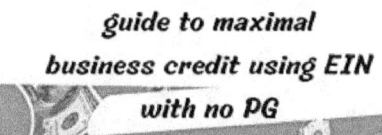

-How to name your business
-Best business structure to get credit
-What information gets reported and where it gets reported
-Companies that extend credit automatically
-How to properly set up your business to receive business credit, even if you have horrible personal credit
-How and when to apply for business bank accounts
-How to pay your Vendors using a credit card even if they do not accept credit cards
-Exactly how and what info to include when you create your business
-Tradelines you should apply for and the specific requirements needed to be accepted
....and so much more!

No chapters! No side notes! No filler! No B.S.!

Get the most credit for your businesses in the least amount of time possible! All delivered in a step-by-step, linear instructional that anyone can follow.

AVAILABLE NOW FROM AMAZON

ALSO
AVAILABLE NOW FROM
AMAZON

Street Smart Money
The Hustler's Guide to Financial Freedom

Unleash your inner hustler and embark on a journey of **financial empowerment** with *"Street Smart Money: The Hustler's Guide to Financial Freedom.* " Join the charismatic and street-savvy

narrator, **Max "Stacks" Johnson**, as he takes you on a wild ride from the gritty streets to financial success.

In this captivating guide, author **Connor Victorious** combines his own transformational journey with the wit and wisdom of **Max "Stacks" Johnson** to provide a fresh **perspective on money management**. Through the lens of **real-life experiences** and **urban slang**, you'll uncover **unorthodox money strategies**, master the art of **budgeting**, learn the ins and outs of **credit scores**, and discover **the power of ethical hustles**.

"Street Smart Money" isn't just about stacking wealth for yourself; it's about building generational prosperity and leaving a lasting legacy. With a focus on **financial literacy**, this guide equips you with the **tools to navigate investments, negotiate deals, and protect your hard-earned money.**

Whether you're a hustler from the streets or simply someone ready to take charge of your financial future, this book offers a unique blend of **inspiration, actionable advice, and a dash of street-smart flavor.** Get ready to embrace the hustle, stack that paper, and prosper like never before.

If you're ready to rewrite your financial story and elevate your wealth-building game, *"Street Smart Money"* is your ultimate companion. Join *Max "Stacks" Johnson and Connor Victorious* as they **empower** you to conquer the world of **personal finance**, one savvy move at a time.

Success is inevitable...

Don't hope. Hustle.

What you can do for someone else, you can do for yourself.

Never work for anyone that isn't YOU.

If you always carry a book with you, you will never be waiting...

Stay tidy. Clutter breeds chaos.

Be prepared to lose it all if you want to succeed.

It truly is lonely at the top...

Life is what you make it. Believe in yourself. There is no such thing as coincidence, God, or luck...you will only succeed if you are able to take responsibility for your mishaps, as well as your achievements.

Be awesome!

Stay amazing!

Love life!

Thank You!

It is difficult for independent writers to get their books acknowledged these days, so if you enjoy "Street Smart Money", please leave a positive review on AMAZON, or type this into your browser to be linked directly:
https://rb.gy/2yduf.

For more about the author and
other services we provide, please visit:
www.felonyfreedomllc.com

We assist with the following:
Easy-to-qualify Business Loans
Business Entity Creation
Paperwork Filing
Business Structuring
EINs, Taxes, and much more...

We are felon-friendly and will assist you any way we can.
Success Is Inevitable - you just have to WANT it bad enough...

www.felonyfreedomllc.com

www.ingramcontent.com/pod-product-compliance
Lightning Source LLC
Chambersburg PA
CBHW062349290526
45794CB00005B/2151